KNOW **GOD**
NO **FEAR**

Christy Wimber is an author, speaker, pioneer, and leader who travels
around the world teaching and encouraging the church.
Her no-nonsense style and honest look at the rewards and challenges
of leadership have led her to encourage and
transform the lives of thousands worldwide.

VISIBLE 20:24
CHESAPEAKE, VA

KNOW **GOD**
NO **FEAR**

You can follow Christy on Facebook, Instagram, Twitter, and Youtube.
christywimber.com

A MESSAGE FROM CHRISTY

Welcome,

I am excited you have decided to journey through this study with me on 'Fear.' This is not a topic I would have liked or even chosen to study through, however, God had other plans.

Unfortunately, Fear is a powerful weapon. We see what's happening in culture today; fear rages through the media, through unhealthy relationships, and countless other ways where the enemy is proving to be 'alive and well.'

I believe it's important to acknowledge the power fear can have, as well as acknowledge how the enemy uses fear to discourage and distract us. *How will we know how to battle if we are not familiar with how the enemy attacks us?* The enemy attacks each of us differently, however, more often than not, **fear** is at the root.

The truth we hold onto, and what you will discover throughout this study, is that we are not alone. Although we acknowledge we have a real enemy, we are also fully aware that God has given us all we need for life and peace.

Each week we will be addressing various topics taken from Genesis 12. We will dissect this text similarly to an exegesis. We will begin with a chapter overview in part 1, then we will dive more deeply into many of the verses in chapter 12. **The video teaching is provided by the QR code that you will find at the beginning of each chapter. This is an unlisted youtube link.**

Watch the video teaching then follow along with this study in your group or individually as we discuss the fear Abram faces before he becomes the patriarch and *father of the faith* we know of today, Abraham.

I want you to understand that it is possible to live in peace. It is possible to fight the onslaught of fear. And it is the way of our God to equip us with all we need. I want you to remember, as you go through this study fears may rise to the surface in your own heart. I realize this can be a bit overwhelming at times, but we cannot change what we do not face. Although I know God will reveal things to you, I also know He will supply the grace you need to face your fears.

Hold onto this truth: God is and will always be, ever so present.

This study book is the companion to the video teaching series. Together they will help you recognize your fears, combat them, and trust *God* more deeply. Throughout each chapter there is time to pause and reflect, as well as a chance to read different translations of scripture, which will deepen your connection to God.

I look forward to hearing the stories of how God has brought freedom and hope to you!

With love,

Christy

Isaiah 41:10, So do not fear, for I am with you; do not be dismayed, for I am your God. I will strengthen you and help you; I will uphold you with my righteous right hand.

TABLE OF CONTENTS

FAITH OVER FEAR

PART 1

The Problem with Fear

Fear is a powerful force.
Fear can upend your world.
Fear can control your mind.
Fear can make you feel crazy.
Fear can paralyze you.

A vast majority of the things we do, or don't do, are motivated by fear. There are hundreds of "phobias" in our vocabulary. Even the average person struggles with the fear of: death, rejection, financial ruin, disease, natural disasters, and even change.

When fear is present it's very hard to recognize what is "real." *Yet, no matter how loud fear can rage, it is never more powerful than the Father.*

 Part 1 Video

Fear & Scripture

While fear has the ability to destroy, faith in God has the ability to overcome. In Scripture, many of our heroes faced scary circumstances. However, their faith and God's love was never ending.

Let's review two scriptures which can strengthen and encourage you no matter the trial.

Psalms 23:4 (NIV)

"EVEN THOUGH I WALK THROUGH THE DARKEST VALLEY,
I WILL FEAR NO EVIL,
FOR YOU ARE WITH ME;
YOUR ROD AND YOUR STAFF,
THEY COMFORT ME."

Isaiah 41:10 (NIV)

"SO DO NOT FEAR, FOR I AM WITH YOU: DO NOT BE DISMAYED, FOR I AM YOUR GOD. I WILL STRENGTHEN YOU AND HELP YOU;
I WILL UPHOLD YOU WITH MY RIGHTEOUS RIGHT HAND."

NO MATTER HOW LOUD FEAR CAN RAGE, IT IS NEVER MORE POWERFUL THAN THE FATHER.

LET'S PAUSE

WHAT IS YOUR GREATEST FEAR?

_____

_____

_____

_____

WHAT DO YOU DO WHEN YOU ARE AFRAID?

_____

_____

_____

_____

HOW HAS FEAR INFLUENCED THE
DECISIONS YOU HAVE MADE?

_____

_____

_____

_____

FAITH OVER FEAR:
THE CHALLENGE OF CHANGE

ABRAM

Change can be a challenge, especially if you find comfort in your surroundings. In Genesis chapter 12, God calls Abram to an uncomfortable future. This calling would be difficult for anyone, however, imagine your call coming at the *young* age of 75! In Genesis 12, God calls Abram to leave his Father's house- this was all he knew, and God was calling him to go to a new land.

This is before Abram's name would be changed to Abraham and Sarai to Sarah.

Let's read the passage together:

Genesis 12:10-20 (WEB)

10 There was a famine in the land. Abram went down into Egypt to live as a foreigner there, for the famine was severe in the land. 11 When he had come near to enter Egypt, he said to Sarai his wife, "See now, I know that you are a beautiful woman to look at. 12 It will happen that when the Egyptians see you, they will say, 'This is his wife.' They will kill me, but they will save you alive. 13 Please say that you are my sister, that it may be well with me for your sake, and that my soul may live because of you."
14 When Abram had come into Egypt, Egyptians saw that the woman was very beautiful. 15 The princes of Pharaoh saw her, and praised her to Pharaoh; and the woman was taken into Pharaoh's house. 16 He dealt well with Abram for her sake. He had sheep, cattle, male donkeys, male servants, female servants, female donkeys, and camels. 17 Yahweh afflicted Pharaoh and his house with great plagues because of Sarai, Abram's wife. 18 Pharaoh called Abram and said, "What is this that you have done to me? Why didn't you tell me that she was your wife? 19 Why did you say, 'She is my sister,' so that I took her to be my wife? Now therefore, see your wife, take her, and go your way."
20 Pharaoh commanded men concerning him, and they escorted him away with his wife and all that he had.

NOTES

_____

_____

_____

THE CHALLENGE OF CHANGE
(CONTINUED)

Abram was to leave his father and his father's household, which was all of his security in many ways. On top of this challenge, Abram faces a famine. The end of verse 10 tells us that this famine was "severe." The Hebrew word חָמוּר translated means burdensome or difficult. It was not uncommon for a region to experience drought. If the rains didn't come when needed, the planting and harvesting was affected.

In the past, Abram was used to a place of abundance. Ur (modern day Iraq), was a port city fed by two rivers which created a rich soil, ultimately leading to great harvests. Canaan, on the other hand, was a place which could experience famine anytime.

Have you ever been in a situation like this...*God asks you to go to a new place, but it's not as comfortable as where you were before?* **Take a moment to write down a time you faced a similar challenge to Abram.**

_____

_____

_____

We are made to grow and the only thing in life we KNOW we can expect—is *change*. This is why faith is required; but every time faith is needed, fear will try to get a foothold. Abram was being called from the familiar and comfortable- to the unknown. Growth in our lives cannot happen without stretching. When things grow it's because stretching is taking place. And Abram was being stretched.

YOU CANNOT HAVE CHANGE WITHOUT SOME PAIN.

WE ARE MADE TO GROW. THE ONLY THING IN LIFE WE KNOW WE CAN EXPECT—IS CHANGE.

FAITH OVER FEAR:
GROWTH & RISK

Growth can be a funny thing. When we're young we can't wait to grow older because we *think* we will have the freedom to do whatever we want. Then, after we become adults, we wish we could go back to our youth! We yearn for the days when we didn't have all the responsibilities we have now, yet: *healthy things grow, healthy things change, and healthy things evolve.* Just as our physical bodies grow with time- our spiritual bodies and our emotional make up should grow, because human beings are called to mature.

Growth is vital in every aspect of our lives: **physically, emotionally and spiritually, we are made to GROW.** The Apostle Paul finds himself frustrated in Hebrews 5:12-13, because the believers were not growing in their faith. He wanted them to "get off milk and move on to meat." But, as we discussed before, we often don't like change, we prefer comfortability. Yet, *God is a God of growth.* Often change will bring challenges and challenges can bring fear. *Every time there is change, fear becomes the enemy's currency.* One of the reasons mature people stop growing and learning is they become less willing to risk failure. **Fear will keep you stagnant.**

Now, let's go back and imagine what Abram thought as he realized the land that the Lord promised to him would not be able to feed him and his family. Imagine the fear of not being able to care for those he loved the most? I wonder what he's thinking: *Did I miss God here? Is this God's will? If this is Gods will, then why am I afraid?* This is why so many stay **stuck**- *the fear of change* is more than the fear of keeping everything the same.

ONE OF THE REASONS WHY MATURE PEOPLE STOP GROWING AND LEARNING IS THEY BECOME LESS WILLING TO RISK FAILURE.

NOTES
_____
_____
_____

Change Invites Challenge

Let's read the promise to Abram in Genesis 12:1-3

God told Abram that he would take care of him and bless him. The promise of blessing and provision had been made. Now the test of Abram's faith is found in his ability to put his **total trust in the promises of God, rather than the fear of walking the promise out.**

1. God promises Abram a **PLACE:** "go to the land that I will show you" (12:1). This is further expanded in the Land covenant found in Deuteronomy 28:8-11.

2. God promises Abram a **PEOPLE:** "I will make you a great nation" (12:2). This is further expanded in the Davidic Covenant found in 2 Samuel 7:8-17.

3. God promises Abram a **BLESSING:** "I will bless those who bless you...." (12:3)

Challenging circumstances will always cause fear, and fear will only undermine our ability to trust God.

Fear causes us to question God's ability to take care of us. However, God's ability should never be in question. The question instead should be: *CAN WE TRUST GOD?*

- The test we face over and over again is- **Which will I allow to rule my heart? Faith or Fear?**

CHALLENGING CIRCUMSTANCES WILL ALWAYS CAUSE FEAR, AND FEAR WILL ONLY UNDERMINE OUR ABILITY TO TRUST GOD...

DO YOU TRUST HIM IN EVERY AREA? WHY OR WHY NOT?

_____

_____

_____

THE ENEMY TO FAITH IS FEAR

Read Genesis 12:10b-16

The first thing to notice in this passage is that *fear,* if not overcome with *faith,* will begin to speak louder than the Father. Let me say this again: *If Fear is not overcome by Faith—it will become louder than our Father.*

Unfortunately, Abram *chooses fear instead of faith,* therefore he functions from that place: *How many know, when pressure comes, we spill. We spill who we are, and we also spill where we put our trust.* When things feel scary who do you turn to first? *Yourself, a friend, or God?* Take some time to ponder past circumstances and to consider how you can put steps in place to trust God FIRST with your uncertainty.

We know from verse 1 it was the Lord who commanded Abram to leave Haran and go to Canaan.

What's missing in this journey is the voice of the Lord telling Abram to go to Egypt. God told Him to go to Ur, *not* to Egypt. Empowered fear can cause panic... which always leads to regret.

The enemy wants to throw whatever he can at you...he wants you to believe you are alone and helpless. Often this causes you to take things into your own hands. Remember a time when your fear turned to panic and then to regret, what spilled out of you?

_____
_____
_____
_____
_____

_____
_____
_____
_____
_____

EMPOWERED FEAR CAN CAUSE PANIC... WHICH ALWAYS LEADS TO REGRET.

LET'S PAUSE

SHARE A TIME YOU EMPOWERED FEAR.

_____
_____
_____
_____

WHAT HAPPENED BECAUSE YOU TOOK THE SITUATION IN YOUR OWN HANDS?

_____
_____
_____
_____

SHARE A TIME WHEN YOU TRUSTED GOD. HOW DID THE SITUATION TURN OUT DIFFERENTLY?

_____
_____
_____

IN OUR OWN HANDS

TRUST HIM TO PROTECT AND PROVIDE

Abram's early actions seem no different than an unbeliever's actions. Abram is acting apart from God and without any trust in God's ability to protect him. Why? Because of fear.

- For Abram, it was the fear of famine which caused his faith to falter and not trust **God's ability to provide for him.** And it was the fear of the Egyptians which caused Abram's faith to falter in **God's ability to protect him from danger.**

Abram would resort to scheming and deception for the purpose of protecting his own life. When we take things into our own hands, we often do things we wouldn't normally do...

Have you ever *responded in panic and fear and thought:* "Oh my gosh these are the best decisions I've ever made!" OF COURSE NOT!

This is when fear becomes the enemy's best weapon, because *fear* can cause you to do the exact opposite of what God wants for your life. Abram ultimately deceives the Egyptians by telling them a half-truth. (There is *some* truth that Abram is Sarai's brother because we are told in chapter twenty that Sarai is Abram's half sister.)

However, Abram was WRONG! And as many of you know...when one lie is told it usually takes many more to cover the initial lie. This perpetual path of lying can cause great pain, regret, and consequence. **Have you ever told a lie which spiraled out of control? How did you learn from it?**

_____

_____

_____

_____

BUT THE LORD...

The Faithfulness of God

In verse 17, we see the faithful Lord intervene—because the Lord had more for Abram than living in a place of fear. As we continue in Genesis, we discover God intervening and sending plagues to Pharaoh and his household. When Abram's faith falters, we discover: **"But the Lord..."** Those three words are a declaration of God's faithfulness. I*n fact, this story of Abram's faltering faith is more about a faithful God than it is about a faithless servant.* We lack faith and have fear like Abram when we are plagued with thoughts such as:

BUT THE LORD
- "I don't have enough money to pay my bills... (But the Lord)
- "My body is in so much pain. (But the Lord)
- "My friends have turned against me. (But the Lord)
- "Our NATION is falling apart." (But the Lord)
- "I am so AFRAID!" (But the Lord)

BUT THE LORD
BUT THE LORD
BUT THE LORD

He is so faithful to deliver us. In Abram we learn of a man who puts himself and his wife in a predicament, BUT the Lord delivers them both unharmed. This is God's faithfulness to deliver his people. He shows Abram mercy and delivers both Abram and Sarai.

If God didn't intervene, would *Abram have stayed in the same place?* Even if we don't understand when God says, "That's enough," His mercy is that we would go forward towards *His* best for our lives.

Name a time when God pushed you out of your comfort zone. What was the result of this leap of faith?

_____

_____

_____

_____

THIS STORY IS LESS ABOUT A FAITHLESS MAN BUT MORE ABOUT A FAITHFUL GOD!

SEE GROW LEARN

SEE:

WHAT SIMILARITIES DO YOU SHARE WITH ABRAM IN GENESIS 12?

GROWTH THIS WEEK:
IS YOUR FEAR LOUDER THAN YOUR FAITH RIGHT NOW?
HOW CAN YOU USE THIS WEEK'S TEACHING
TO SILENCE YOUR FEARS?

_____

_____

_____

_____

_____

_____

_____

LEARN:
TAKE SOME TIME TO REREAD AND PRAY THROUGH THE SCRIPTURES
BELOW. COMPARE TRANSLATIONS- IS THERE A SPECIFIC
TRANSLATION THAT YOU IDENTIFY WITH MORE? HOW IS GOD
SPEAKING TO YOU AS YOU STUDY HIS WORD?

PSALM 23:4

ISAIAH 41:10

NO FEAR OF FAILURE
PART 2

Quick Review

In part 1, we discover that Genesis 12 shares the promises told to the father of our faith, Abram. Yet, his story is less about a faithful man but more about a FAITHFUL God. The grace of God pours over Abram. Although he makes many mistakes out of fear, God never leaves or forsakes him. **What was the most important point you walked away with last week?**

_____

_____

_____

_____

Pause.

Take some time in prayer before we venture forward. Ask God to show you places of fear that are holding you back. Then, ask the Lord to mend those broken places.

 Part 2 Video

Worship First

Let's look back at Genesis 12:8 together:

Genesis 12:8 (NIV)
FROM THERE HE WENT ON TOWARD THE HILLS EAST OF BETHEL AND PITCHED HIS TENT, WITH BETHEL ON THE WEST AI ON THE EAST. THERE HE BUILT AN ALTAR TO THE LORD AND CALLED ON THE NAME OF THE LORD.

Abram in verse 8, took a moment to pause and spend time in Worship to the Lord. Even during this hilltop experience it would only take a few days before Abram got off track and faced incredible challenges.

Often times when I experience God's power in Worship, it seems almost instantly I begin to face a frightening and challenging time in my life. In fact some of our most vulnerable times to temptation is after a spiritually high point in our lives. **Take a moment to reflect on your own experiences. Have you experienced this as well?**

FACE THE FEAR OF THE UNKNOWN

ABRAM

The unknown is often scary, this was something Abram learned quickly. God asked him to leave the security of his father and his father's household. Before his father had chosen to stop in Haran—they lived in Ur. As we discussed last week, Ur was a place of great abundance. Canaan didn't compare to Ur when it came to comfort. Ur was a port city, while Canaan was a place that could succumb to famine at any time. This is what pushing through the fear of the unknown looks like: *It looks like giving up the familiar. Fear loves to haunt people with the unfamiliar.* This is when fear leans into doubt and you can find yourself asking these types of questions, (which more than likely also plagued the mind of Abram):

- How do you know it was God who spoke to you?
- Why in the world would you leave something so good and comfortable?
- Don't you think it's stupid to leave your security?
- Why would you move away from your family?
- Why would you give up your job?

While these questions and doubts may flood your mind, you can still choose to trust in God because: *We cannot grow without change… and we cannot change…without pain.*

Philippians 3:14 (NLT)
"I PRESS ON TO REACH THE END OF THE RACE AND RECEIVE THE HEAVENLY PRIZE FOR WHICH GOD, THROUGH CHRIST JESUS, IS CALLING US."

"I press on," diōkō, means to run after, to follow to seek after, to be persecuted, to be treated harshly. In fact, it means, "to face persecution is to be on the right track." It's the same promise as:

Matthew 5:10 (KJV)
"BLESSED ARE THEY WHICH ARE PERSECUTED FOR RIGHTEOUSNESS' SAKE: FOR THEIRS IS THE KINGDOM OF HEAVEN."

NOTES
_____
_____
_____

Run the Race

NO RUNNER BEGINS A RACE NOT INTENDING TO FINISH

Who does Jesus say has the Kingdom of heaven in Matthew 5:10? The word "persecuted" in Matthew and the word "press" in Philippians have the same meaning. They mean, "to suffer." We often want to receive a reward without having to run the race, however, victory and break through come only through participation. No runner begins a race not intending to finish. We're in this race of faith with the intention to finish well. However, just like Abram, many times God may lead us unto paths that don't make any sense. This means we have to give up control and trust God to guide us. Take some group time to share a time in your life when you took a leap of faith that seemed to make no sense to you or those around you. How difficult is it for you to give up control?

No one wants to enter into a race they know they will fail. This is the space in which fear loves to override your mind. You may begin to question yourself with thoughts like, "If I step into the unknown, what if I fail?" We love and rely on security.

My son like most children, found comfort in his security blanket. He never wanted to let it go. However, healthy things grow! Imagine if I allowed my son to continue through grade school and high school with his blanket, it would have been a disaster for him. *Familiarity can often crush maturity.* Growth doesn't come from what was, it comes from the exploration of new places and new experiences.

Name a time in your life when you were able to let go of something comfortable and in turn found a greater path forward.

_____

_____

_____

_____

_____

FAMINE

Abram faces famine

Last week we discussed just how difficult it must have been for Abram as he walked away from a land of plenty, to a land in the midst of famine. So many questions must have filled his mind as he considered how he was going to take care of his family.

Unfortunately, many of us have famines we struggle with internally.

- The fear of not having enough food.
- The fear of not having enough money.
- A trigger from your past which prevents forward motion.

The list is different for everyone. Yet, we all have to recognize these places of famine we hold within. The ones which keep us captive and paralyzed with fear. In Genesis 12, famine, rāʿāb̲. Waa-Av means, "a hunger and afraid of death."

Do you have enough?

Here's the thing, Abram faces this famine after he makes the decision to follow God. Life didn't become perfect for him, matter of fact, it got more difficult. Abram listened to God and stepped out in faith even though he had the added responsibility of providing for his household.

Many of us have the responsibility of family just like Abram. This gives way to a fear of failure because it's not just about you. Realistically, most of us have more than enough. There's a reason phrases such as, "keeping up with the Joneses" is popular. We have to ask ourselves regularly, "*Where does the pull to want more come from?*" Peter warns us in 1 Peter:

1 Peter 2:11 (NLT)

"DEAR FRIENDS, I WARN YOU AS TEMPORARY RESIDENTS AND FOREIGNERS' TO KEEP AWAY FROM WORLDLY DESIRES THAT WAGE WAR AGAINST YOUR VERY SOULS."

LET'S PAUSE

IDENTIFY THE FAMINE IN YOUR OWN LIFE.

_____

_____

_____

_____

HOW IMPORTANT ARE MATERIAL THINGS? CAN YOU IDENTIFY ANYTHING THAT YOU HOLD TOO TIGHTLY?

_____

_____

_____

_____

HOW LIKELY ARE YOU TO FOLLOW GOD'S LEADING, EVEN IF IT MEANS AN UNCOMFORTABLE EXISTENCE?

_____

_____

_____

BE AT THE CENTER OF GOD'S WILL

We often confuse obeying God with an easy life, however, Abram and Sarai show us just how difficult it can be to trust and obey God. At this point in our Scripture, Abram is in the early stages of his journey and he has made some really terrible mistakes. Yet, he still trusts God, and as he goes forward in his journey, he consistently strives to be at the center of God's will. Often we glamorize a faithful servant who follows rightly after God. However, being in the center of God's will doesn't mean there aren't challenges–or that fear will no longer be present. As westerners, we think if we are at the center of God's will then life will be easy. We assume the enemy will not attack us and we can continue living the "western dream." The truth is, when God is present miracles happen! Unfortunately, in order for miracles to take place, the enemy must be active. He will haunt and distract us with fearful scenarios which cause us to repeatedly need faith. But God will never leave us as we discover in Psalms 23.

Psalm 23:5 (KJV)

"YOU PREPARE A TABLE FOR ME IN THE MIDST OF MY ENEMIES."

In Psalm 23:5, we learn that God has set a table for us in the center of His will. Yet, the enemy is all around! We need to decide whether to focus on fellowship with God...or be fearful because the enemy will come after us. Let's take some time to read and meditate on the first 5 verses of the well known Psalm 23. As you reflect, take time to remember that God is your provider, Jehovah Jireh. He promises to never leave you behind.

Psalm 23 (KJV)

"THE LORD IS MY SHEPHERD; I SHALL NOT WANT.
HE MAKETH ME TO LIE DOWN IN GREEN PASTURES: HE LEADETH ME BESIDE THE STILL WATERS.
HE RESTORETH MY SOUL: HE LEADETH ME IN THE PATHS OF RIGHTEOUSNESS FOR HIS NAME'S SAKE. YEA, THOUGH I WALK THROUGH THE VALLEY OF THE SHADOW OF DEATH, I WILL FEAR NO EVIL: FOR THOU ART WITH ME; THY ROD AND THY STAFF THEY COMFORT ME.
THOU PREPAREST A TABLE BEFORE ME IN THE PRESENCE OF MINE ENEMIES:
THOU ANOINTEST MY HEAD WITH OIL; MY CUP RUNNETH OVER."

NOTES
_____
_____
_____

SEE GROW LEARN

SEE:

HOW DOES YOUR TABLE LOOK AS YOU REFLECT ON PSALM 23:5?

GROWTH THIS WEEK:
WOULD YOU SAY THAT YOU ARE CURRENTLY IN THE CENTER OF
GOD'S WILL? WHY OR WHY NOT?

_____

_____

_____

_____

_____

_____

_____

LEARN:
TAKE SOME TIME TO REREAD AND PRAY THROUGH THE SCRIPTURES
BELOW. COMPARE TRANSLATIONS- IS THERE A SPECIFIC
TRANSLATION THAT YOU IDENTIFY WITH MORE? HOW IS GOD
SPEAKING TO YOU AS YOU STUDY HIS WORD?

PSALMS 23	PHILIPPIANS 3:14

DON'T PANIC IN FEAR

PART 3

Quick Review

In part 2, we discussed the fear of failure and the fear of not having enough. These fears can hold us prisoner from God's best for our lives. However, God's best doesn't always feel comfortable. Yet, the growth, break through, and maturity makes it all *worth it*. **Identify a time when you felt uncomfortable, but looking back you realize it was an important turning point in your life?**

_____

_____

_____

_____

Pause.

Take some time in prayer before we venture forward. Ask God to show you a time in your life where you had a child like faith. Then, ask the Lord to help grow your faith for today.

Part 3 Video

From Worshipper to Schemer

As we discovered in Genesis 12, Abram takes time to worship the Lord and set up an altar to honor him. Then, almost immediately after his mountain top experience, Abram faces a famine. This obstacle led to a landmine in Abram's mind: as fear set in, *panic began to take over*. Abram begins to scheme and take his situation into his own hands by going to Egypt.

This week our goal is to learn from Abram by discovering our own response to fear and panic. **Have you experienced a time that you panicked and made a scheme to get yourself out of the situation? How did that situation turn out for you? How would you have handled it differently today?**

_____

_____

_____

_____

_____

_____

PRESSURE REVEALS HOW WE THINK

As fear and panic take over, pressure begins to build. We often have conversations in our heads when we plot our survival in high stress scenarios. You may have experienced a conversation with yourself that went a bit like this: *"Well, if this happens... then I'll do this. But if that happens, I'll do that instead."* Your immediate thought was not prayer, but instead how you could control the situation.

Can't you picture Abram in this part of our Scripture, Genesis 12:9-13? As the pressure builds for him to take care of his family in the midst of a famine, he begins to scheme for a successful existence in Egypt. Unfortunately, instead of seeking God when the pressure mounted...Abram spilled a scheme that was not of God.

IF OUR THINKING ABOUT GOD IS OFF, THEN EVERYTHING IS OFF.

Often, pressure pushes to the surface who we are...and not who we'd like to be. **What is your normal response to pressure? Are you someone who thrives in those moments or does something else spill out of you?**

_____

_____

_____

Pressure also gives us a glimpse into how healthy or unhealthy our thinking is...what are we feeding our minds and what do we believe about ourselves? Remember Abram is walking into a new season in his life that is filled with promise. God promised him countless descendants, a father of nations, yet, he forgot his inheritance and instead lived in the panic of the moment. He allowed fear to interfere and make him forget all the Lord had spoken to him. If we believe fear and think God will not come through for us– then we have given the enemy exactly what he wants. *If our thinking about God is off, then everything is off!*

PRESSURE PUSHES TO THE SURFACE WHO WE ARE...AND NOT WHO WE'D LIKE TO BE.

24

Pressure Can Create Panic

AND PANIC EMPOWERS FEAR

BUT, Romans 8:6 (NIV) says:
THE MIND GOVERNED BY THE FLESH IS DEATH, BUT THE MIND GOVERNED BY THE SPIRIT IS LIFE AND PEACE.
Is your life marked by peace? Sometimes we have to fight for our peace. We have to have the determination to choose peace by stepping outside of our circumstances to hear what God says. Ultimately, 99% of the battle is in our minds. Take some group time to share a time in your life when you took a leap of faith that seemed to make no sense to you or those around you... *What resonated most in this discussion time?*

_____

_____

_____

How difficult is it for you to give up control?

_____

_____

_____

Name a time in your life when you were able to let go of something comfortable and in turn found a greater path forward.

_____

_____

_____

_____

We have to have the determination to choose peace by stepping outside of our circumstances to hear what God says.

25

FAMINE:
Abram Chooses Fear

God had been very specific in his directions, He said, "get up and go and I will show you where I'm sending you." But Abram decides to take a detour when faced with famine. **Go back and reread verse 10**. Abram's fear of the famine and fear of what he's going to encounter causes him to sin and make decisions outside of somebody who's going to be entrusted with nations. We know from verse 1, it was the Lord who commanded Abram to leave Haran and go to Canaan.

So, what's missing in this journey?

_____

The voice of the Lord is missing. God told Him to go to UR, but God did **NOT** tell him to go to Egypt.

We can tell from this passage that Abram was trying to avoid pain and any possibility of facing hardship. As a society we hate pain and we hate change. We live in a world that tries to avoid pain at any cost. Just think about all of the escapism in our culture today, we look to numb pain and avoid facing our reality.

But you can't escape and numb yourself and still learn the life lessons meant for you.

Abram was in a season of training. God is training you, and training only comes with sweat, tears, and hardship. _We cannot change what we do not choose to face_. And when God is forming us, it takes us outside of our comfort zones. Which is why we have the Holy Spirit, who is our comforter. The gift of the comforter obviously tells us that we are going to be _uncomfortable!_ Which is why we have the power to stay and face hardship. God is not asking us to do this alone! He is our provider and has provided us with the help we need.

- Muscles are made in strain
- Diamonds are made in heat & fire
- Pure gold in extreme heat

Our testimonies worth sharing all came at a cost. Without the trial, there would be no testimony or no need for a miracle. There is a great quote that says, "Christians have bumper stickers and catch phrases, believers have creeds and promises, disciples have scars and stories."

WHEN FEAR OVER FAITH=FLESH

As we remain in verse 10, we see Abram comes up with his own plan. Abram acts outside of God- and instead operates in the flesh, because fear has gotten so loud he's panicking! **Fear gives power to the flesh!** I will continue to repeat this: *fear*, if not overcome with faith, will begin to speak louder than the Father.

2 Timothy 1:7 (NIV)
"FOR THE SPIRIT GOD GAVE US DOES NOT MAKE US TIMID, BUT GIVES US POWER, LOVE AND SELF-DISCIPLINE."

However, I understand that for many anxiety is a real thing. Often it's a chemical imbalance which may even cause uncontrollable panic attacks. My intention is not to undermine how debilitating it can be for you on a daily basis. Remember, God has not given you a spirit of fear, but of love and discipline, which means, "of sound mind". So let me encourage those of you who have to fight just to get out of bed. You may not be able to do much, but just showing up is a victory. It was Francis of Assisi, who said, "Start by doing what's necessary; then do what's possible; and suddenly you are doing the impossible." Keep taking those small steps daily, and give yourself credit when you find the strength to be present. Most importantly, remember you do not have to do this alone.

Paul used three verbs to describe our relationship with the Spirit. Open your Bible and read **Galatians 5:16-25.**

- He called us to walk in the Spirit (v. 16), which requires us to be led by the Spirit (v.18)
- To live in or by the Spirit (v. 25). [Walk- Led & Live]

Here are some practical steps based off of Paul's letter to the Galations:

First, walk in the Spirit;
Second, be led by the Spirit (Gal. 5:24; Rom. 8:14)
Third, live in the Spirit and let your whole being come alive by the Spirit (Gal. 5:25).

NOTES
_____
_____
_____

LET'S PAUSE

ARE THERE THINGS YOU DO IN ORDER TO NUMB
YOUR EMOTIONS? WHY?

_____

_____

_____

_____

WHAT DOES IT LOOK LIKE FOR YOU TO 'WALK
WITH THE SPIRIT?'

_____

_____

_____

_____

DO YOU STRUGGLE WITH ANXIETY? IF SO,
WHAT ARE SOME OF YOUR DAILY
ACCOMPLISHMENTS? LIST THEM BELOW.

_____

_____

_____

Be Led by God

TO BE LED BY GOD IS TO BE LED INTO THE PURPOSES OF GOD

Romans 8:14 (NIV) says,

"FOR THOSE WHO ARE LED BY THE SPIRIT OF GOD ARE THE CHILDREN OF GOD."

What we're led into, is how we can tell what– and who is leading us. *The enemy only has one plan: steal, kill & destroy!* Not only is the enemy the thief, but he has a plan to mislead and misguide. Everything the enemy touches gets destroyed. Every effort he puts towards you is meant to destroy you. **The Hebrew name for Satan is *Abaddon*, which means "Destruction."** Pressure and panic brought out the sinful stuff in Abram. Every day we have to make the decision on where we're going to live from– *the spirit of God or our sinful nature.*

Romans 7:25 (NIV)

"THANKS BE TO GOD, WHO DELIVERS ME THROUGH JESUS CHRIST OUR LORD! SO THEN, I MYSELF IN MY MIND AM A SLAVE TO GOD'S LAW, BUT IN MY SINFUL NATURE A SLAVE TO THE LAW OF SIN."

Unhealthy fear is never the Lord. Knowing this truth is the one thing I have held onto. Anything that has fear attached to it– is never God. This truth is so deep within me that it has become a root of peace. I recognize this peace, and it helps me understand if I am on track with God. God has more for you, and as it is with any change that has deep potential: the enemy will do whatever he can to stop you. You have to ask yourself, **'Who has the most to gain by me gaining less of God?'** Make this decision for yourself:
"I will not allow the enemy to have his way with me in any area of my life any longer." Abram had to face his fears. In fact all of the great men and women of the Bible, and those who have made history, have had to confront their fears. By confronting their fears, fear no longer had power over them or their future.

SEE GROW LEARN

SEE:
NAME TWO WAYS YOU RECOGNIZE THE ENEMY OPERATING IN YOUR LIFE.

GROWTH THIS WEEK:
HAVE YOU EVER EXPERIENCED A TIME WHEN YOU DID THE OPPOSITE OF WHAT YOU KNOW GOD INSTRUCTED? WHAT WAS THE OUTCOME?

_____

_____

_____

_____

_____

_____

_____

LEARN:
TAKE SOME TIME TO REREAD AND PRAY THROUGH THE SCRIPTURES BELOW. COMPARE TRANSLATIONS- IS THERE A SPECIFIC TRANSLATION THAT YOU IDENTIFY WITH MORE? HOW IS GOD SPEAKING TO YOU AS YOU STUDY HIS WORD?

2 TIMOTHY 1:7

ROMANS 7:25

THE PROMISES OF GOD

PART 4

Quick Review

In Part 3, we talked about how fear can get us to operate from a place of panic, pressure, and even pain. Abram had to face his fears in order to move forward, but when he panicked and acted from a place of fear his sinful nature took over. If we don't allow God's voice to be the loudest and most important, our own fears begin to lead our thoughts and actions. What are some ways you were able to overcome fear this week?

_____

_____

_____

_____

Pause.
Take some time in prayer before we venture forward. Ask God to remind you of different moments in which He answered your prayers. Do you feel He keeps His promises to you? Be honest with Him in this time.

 Part 4 Video

The Promise

Today we are going to focus on the promises of God. There are over 7,000 promises in the Bible. Isn't that amazing? Why would God give us so many promises– because He *knows us,* and He knows when faced with the pressures of life we can be forgetful. His promises are reminders that He is always with us.

Now, let's look back at the beginning of Genesis 12 and the promises God made to Abram:

- God promises Abram a PLACE "go to the land that I will show you" (12:1). This is further expanded in the Land covenant found in Deuteronomy 28:8-11.

- God promises Abram a PEOPLE "I will make of you a great nation" (12:2). This is further expanded in the Davidic Covenant found in 2 Samuel 7:8-17.

- God promises Abram a BLESSING "I will bless those who bless you...." (12:3)

GOD PROMISES ABRAM A PLACE

God loves you and cares for every aspect of your life. Everything that matters to you matters to Him, including where you live. We are told:

Psalm 68:6 (NIV)
"GOD SETS THE LONELY IN FAMILIES..."

God calls each of us to places where we will encounter His blessing. God cares so much that He asks us to pray for our cities, because when the city is blessed, it blesses us:

2 Chronicles 6:34 (NIV)
"WHEN YOUR PEOPLE GO TO WAR AGAINST THEIR ENEMIES, WHEREVER YOU SEND THEM, AND WHEN THEY PRAY TO YOU TOWARD THIS CITY YOU HAVE CHOSEN AND THE TEMPLE I HAVE BUILT FOR YOUR NAME"

WHEN GOD IS MOVING YOU FORWARD, DON'T GET DISTRACTED BY FEAR.

In verse 12:1, God calls Abram to a new land, a place where his blessing will be. God asked Abram to leave all that was familiar to him, his home, his relatives, and his native country. Abram had it pretty good where he was, but God had better plans for him. Often fear will keep you from stepping out of your comfort zone and moving forward. When God is moving you forward, don't allow yourself to be distracted by fear. Challenging circumstances will always cause fear which only undermines our ability to trust God. Fear causes us to question God's ability to take care of us, but His ability is never in question. **Are you in the place where God has called you? Is there anything holding you back from going forward into the place of promise for your life?**

_____

_____

_____

God Promises Abram a People

In verse 12:2, God promises to Abram a great nation. In this new place he is being entrusted to lead a people and to become the spiritual father of the faith. Not all of us are called to lead a nation, but we are called to people. We are not made to do life alone. God calls us into families, both in the natural and the spiritual sense. **Ask yourself, who are your people? Who are your tribe?**

It's easy to miss the fullness of God's promises when we get stuck in familiar relationships. Even though they might be great, fear can keep us from meeting someone new. God often asks us to step out, calling us to new people. This is a place where God stretches and grows us. A new relationship can bring new life to us. I've experienced God's promises over my life with new relationships that have made my life richer.

I went through a season where I had to learn who my people were. Sometimes we stay in relationships out of obligation or fear that we will never meet anyone new, but our relational history should never feel like a future obligation. There is a difference between loyalty and slavery in relationships. Your relationships should move you toward health and freedom and not stem from past obligations or fear. Fear can tell you, "you'll be all alone" or, "you'll never find new friends". This is the enemy trying to keep us from a new life, but remember, there is a whole world out there and God is calling you forward. Loyalty is freedom. Obligation is slavery. **Is fear the reason why you don't have new relationships?**

What if we didn't have missionaries who were willing to sacrifice so that other people would know Jesus? As a believer in Jesus, a missionary is not only called to a place...but to a people.

LOYALTY IS FREEDOM. OBLIGATION IS SLAVERY.

GOD PROMISES ABRAM A BLESSING

Here in verse 12:3, God makes His promise of blessing to Abram. He tells him that He will bless those that bless him and curse those that curse him. These are strong words!

Blessing is a word that Christians use often but there is much more meaning behind it than you might realize. In Hebrew the word for bless is barak ברך. Here, the word bless means abundance, prosperity, and praise. It also means a treaty of peace and a promise of freedom. God is saying that when you are in the place and with the people of your anointing, there is an inner peace that comes over your life.

In Hebrew the word for curse is arar ארר. It means to not have the hand of God upon your life– *isn't that scary?* But God promises to go before you… that is the blessing of divine favor over your life.

God is a God that wants to bless you. If He is moving you forward, it's because what you have now is not God's best for you. It's worth the blessings He has for you to push past the fear and uncertainty. On the other side of fear, you will find abundance.

God makes a promise to us… We must choose to persevere and get through the problems in order to get to the promise! God leads us forward into life and peace where we are free. *Who doesn't want that?*

Take some time and write down at least three blessings you have experienced in your life.

_____

_____

_____

Hebrews 11: 8-9 (NIV)
BY FAITH ABRAHAM, WHEN CALLED TO GO TO A PLACE HE WOULD LATER RECEIVE AS HIS INHERITANCE, OBEYED AND WENT, EVEN THOUGH HE DID NOT KNOW WHERE HE WAS GOING. BY FAITH HE MADE HIS HOME IN THE PROMISED LAND LIKE A STRANGER IN A FOREIGN COUNTRY; HE LIVED IN TENTS, AS DID ISAAC AND JACOB, WHO WERE HEIRS WITH HIM OF THE SAME PROMISE.

Habakkuk 2:2 (NKJV)
THEN THE LORD ANSWERED ME AND SAID: "WRITE THE VISION AND MAKE IT PLAIN ON TABLETS, THAT HE MAY RUN WHO READS IT"

SEE GROW LEARN

SEE:
SPEND SOME TIME IDENTIFYING THE BLESSINGS OF YOUR CURRENT COMMUNITY.

GROWTH THIS WEEK:
WHAT IS HOLDING YOU BACK FROM MOVING FORWARD AND EMBRACING ALL GOD HAS FOR YOU?

_____

_____

_____

_____

_____

_____

_____

_____

LEARN:
TAKE SOME TIME TO REREAD AND PRAY THROUGH THE SCRIPTURES BELOW. COMPARE TRANSLATIONS– IS THERE A SPECIFIC TRANSLATION THAT YOU IDENTIFY WITH MORE? HOW IS GOD SPEAKING TO YOU AS YOU STUDY HIS WORD?

2 CHRONICLES 6:34	HEBREWS 11:8-9

GOD CAN USE ANYONE

PART 5

Quick Review

I hope you took some time last week to think about the promises God made to Abram and write down the promises God has made over your life. Remembering the promises God has spoken over us, is key to staying focused and not allowing ourselves to be guided by fear. In Part 4, we talked about how God calls us to places and people, and how His blessing of abundance, peace, and life is found in our obedience to trust Him, wherever he leads us. **Did you recognize his blessings in your life this week?**

The Unexpected Person

In today's lesson we're going to discuss how God can use anyone to remind us that He is God, and even turn us around from a bad decision. Too often we put God in a box and expect Him to use the same people in the same ways to speak to us. In fact, we find many times in scripture where God uses an unexpected person to move His people in the right direction. **Take some time to reflect on the people who you allow to speak into your life. Is God's voice the loudest?**

_____

_____

_____

_____

Pause.

Take some time in prayer before we venture forward. In your prayer time, release your insecurities. Do you feel that you are unworthy of His love or for Him to use you? Ask Him to show you how *HE SEES YOU.*

 Part 5 Video

DISOBEDIENCE GIVES FEAR PERMISSION

Take a moment to reread Genesis 12:14-16. In these verses Abram is panicking and making decisions from a place of fear and disobedience; therefore, opening the door to the enemy. The choices he's made have given fear permission, empowering it even more. His wife is taken by Pharaoh, and he plans to make her his wife. In turn Abram receives gifts, seemingly rewarding him for his lies. *It might look, from the outside, like Abram is being blessed but these blessings are not from God.*

WE MAKE DECISIONS FROM ONE OF TWO KINGDOMS: EITHER FROM THE SPIRIT OF GOD OR FROM SIN AND THE ENEMY.

Abram's fear of not having enough is what lead to his disobedience, and now he's sold himself out for money. Money can be powerful. If you have a fear of not having enough, it's hard to know how you will respond– *unless you've dealt with the root of that fear.*

We all have different fears the enemy uses against us. The enemy can't create, but he can take your fears and use them against you. If we don't get to the roots of our deepest fears and heal them, grounded in God, the enemy will trigger those fears. This can cause us to make choices from fear rather than faith. When we panic and make decisions from the kingdom of the enemy, whatever we obtain will not be protected by God. **How do you go about making decisions? Are they mainly out of fear or faith?**

_____

_____

_____

DISOBEDIENCE
(CONTINUED)

1 Timothy 6:10 (KJV)
"FOR THE LOVE OF MONEY IS THE ROOT OF ALL EVIL."

It's not money itself that's evil, but rather- the motivation behind wanting more that can become a sin. **How do you approach money and material things? Do you struggle with being fearful that you never have enough?**

_____

_____

_____

Just because we have more doesn't mean it's a blessing. I'm a big believer in tithing because everything we have that is good is from God. Giving back to God puts protection around us and our money. **What is your approach to giving to the Lord?**

_____

_____

_____

James 1:17 (NIV)
"EVERY GOOD AND PERFECT GIFT IS FROM ABOVE, COMING DOWN FROM THE FATHER OF THE HEAVENLY LIGHTS."

God is the giver of gifts, Jehovah Jirah, the Great Provider. God promises to provide for us, but He doesn't promise the way He will provide. He wants us to put our trust in Him and not focus on the way in which we will receive His gifts. **Write down a time when you saw the Lord provide for you in an unexpected way. It does not need to be a financial time but any time you felt His provision for you.**

_____

_____

_____

_____

_____

_____

But the Lord...

In verse 17, we find the words, *But The LORD*. It may not look like it, but God has been watching Abram, He has seen what Abram's lies have produced, and is about to intervene. Like Abram, God gives you and I free will. We have a choice in what we're going to do with our lives. Just because God hasn't intervened doesn't mean He's ok with your decisions. Often it seems God doesn't intervene right away because He wants us to get what we *think* we want. By allowing this, we can discover for ourselves it wasn't at all what we thought it would be. Sometimes God allows things to continue to give us more exposure. Then we can see very clearly what has been corrupted, allowing for the root to be exposed.

Proverbs 20:23 (NIV)

"THE LORD DETESTS DIFFERING WEIGHTS, AND DISHONEST SCALES DO NOT PLEASE HIM."

God sometimes doesn't intervene because...

1. His Mercy

2. He's allowing for more exposure

Remember, Abram is not in the place he is supposed to be, and his old ways of sin have caught up with him. His fear of not having enough has led him to make these poor choices. God has allowed him to dig a hole just enough so that when He intervenes it will be undeniable. There are consequences to Abrams' choices. Having consequences doesn't mean that God isn't merciful. It just means that we can't do whatever we want and not have repercussions. We also shouldn't confuse consequences with warfare. Not everything we go through is the enemy's fault, it is simply the consequences of the choices we've made. Now, because of Abram's choices, Sarai has lost her honor and Pharaoh's household is experiencing a plague. Often, we fail to see the damage we do to others because of our wrong choices and actions. It would almost seem as though Abram's choices are having more impact on others than on him.

But the Lord... (continued)

Abram is getting so much from Pharaoh: animals, money, and invitations to the palace. He confuses the things he's getting with God's blessings, but he is completely out of fellowship with God. Before he left for Egypt he was worshipping and calling upon the name of the Lord. The Lord was appearing to him and speaking to him personally. Now, Abram's worshipping has ceased, and the Lord is silent. **Have you experienced a time when you felt God was silent in your life? Did you have a break through time with the Lord?**

Don't let the fear of what you *don't have* allow you to settle for what you *know* isn't the Lord. At the end of the day, it's not worth it– if it's not from God. No matter how great it seems– if it's not from God, *you don't want it*. It's important to have a healthy fear of the Lord. **Fear, meaning conviction, not condemnation.** Some of you have been taught that God is waiting to condemn you when you make poor choices. However, as we discover in this passage; even when Abram fails, God, in His mercy, puts him back on track by using a pagan to speak to him. **Try and remember a time when wisdom came from a place you least expected. How did you respond?**

_____

_____

_____

_____

_____

_____

_____

_____

GOD CAN USE ANYONE

PHARAOH

Amid all the mistruths and deceit, we discover someone unexpected who understands the gravity of what is going on: *PHARAOH*

- A disease strikes Pharaoh's household as a consequence of Sarai being there.

In the ancient world, they believed that disease or sickness occurred as a direct result of displeasure on the part of a god. The pagan religions saw disease and sickness as a direct result of sin. The Lord revealed to Pharaoh that Sarai was Abram's wife and as a result, the Lord struck Pharaoh and his household with disease. Pharaoh does not question God... He believes and calls Abram to him and begins to rebuke him for what he's done.

- The Lord uses a pagan ruler to rebuke Abram; *twice* Pharaoh asks Abram why he lied to him.
- It's sad but sometimes unbelievers can recognize the works of God even before His own people!

The Lord revealed to Pharaoh that Sarai was Abram's wife and as a result the Lord struck Abram's household with disease. The amazing thing is that Pharaoh doesn't doubt or question, he believes. Once pharaoh realizes what has happened, he obeys God, and Abram is spared. Imagine what takes place in the mind of Pharaoh when he finds out that Abram, a servant of the one true God purposefully lied and tried to deceive him? We must remember, God can use anyone at any time for His purposes.

Proverbs 21:1 (NKJV)
"THE KINGS HEART IS IN THE HANDS OF THE LORD; LIKE THE RIVERS OF WATER- HE TURNS IT WHENEVER HE WISHES."

NOTES
_____

_____

_____

SEE GROW LEARN

SEE:

GOD CAN USE ANYONE! HOW CAN HE USE YOU THIS WEEK?

GROWTH THIS WEEK:
WHAT ARE YOUR FEARS? WRITE THEM DOWN BUT THEN END EACH
FEAR WITH ... BUT THE LORD!

_____

_____

_____

_____

_____

_____

_____

LEARN:

TAKE SOME TIME TO REREAD AND PRAY THROUGH THE SCRIPTURES
BELOW. COMPARE TRANSLATIONS- IS THERE A SPECIFIC
TRANSLATION THAT YOU IDENTIFY WITH MORE? HOW IS GOD
SPEAKING TO YOU AS YOU STUDY HIS WORD?

PROVERBS 20:23

PROVERBS 21:1

PRAISE DEFEATS FEAR
PART 6

Quick Review

Our study is coming to a close and I've thoroughly enjoyed going verse by verse with you in Genesis, chapter 12. We have witnessed the weaknesses in Abram in which he often operated from a place of fear rather than faith. Consequently, leading him to learn some things the hard way.

I'm sure that during our weeks together God has brought up different things inside of you. He wants to use the story of Abram to bring you to a wholeness and healing in Him. God doesn't want you to live in fear.

Pause.

Take some time in prayer before we venture forward. In your prayer time, ask the Lord to reveal areas He wants to heal in your heart in regards to fear.

 Part 6 Video

An Altar

Early on in chapter 12, when Abram first traveled through the land of Canaan, it says in verse 7, 'the Lord appeared to him and promised Abram the land for his offspring.' Immediately, Abram built an altar to the Lord.

All throughout the Old Testament we find when God moved on his people, they would often stop and build an altar to God. These altars represented places of worship and places of remembrance. They were reminders of all God had done. And when something was represented as a place of remembrance, they became places where the people would stop in gratitude and worship God. **Are there places that remind you of God's goodness which will cause you to stop and worship Him in gratitude?**

_____

_____

_____

_____

OUR LIFE IS AN ALTAR

Altars represent a place of remembrance, a reminder, where we also find our response.

- Altars were often made of stones. They often mean 'uncut stones'
- Stones represent *remembrance*.

All of us have an altar to the Lord. *Your life is an altar to the Lord*. The stones we use to build the altar are those hard things in our life where we overcame and experienced victory (a time when God showed up and visited us in the midst of great hardship).

Consider every time God has revealed Himself to you, when He has healed you, restored you, rescued and saved you. Do you remember what He's done? Remember each of these things and imagine them as stones to place upon your altar.

Our altars also represent the joyous times, in every season, there has been another stone to place on your altar.

However, altars are also corporate. Those of you participating in this study as a church—notice that your church has an altar. Every time your church family has sacrificed time, spread Christ's love, and shared the Gospel you have placed another stone on that altar. The altar releases a fragrance to the Lord and it forms our fragrance of worship and becomes an altar of worship to our God. Your life is a living altar to the Lord. King David said, "I refuse to offer anything to God that costs me nothing..."

The God that's revealed Himself to you in the past, is the same God who wants to lead you into your future.

HOW DOES PRAISE DEFEAT FEAR?

I quickly want to look forward into scripture at a time when Jehoshaphat, (son of Asa, descendant of David) used praise to defeat fear. Let's move for a short time into 2 Chronicles.

2 Chronicles 17:3-6,
"THE LORD WAS WITH JEHOSHAPHAT BECAUSE HE FOLLOWED THE WAYS OF HIS FATHER DAVID BEFORE HIM. HE DID NOT CONSULT THE BAALS BUT SOUGHT THE GOD OF HIS FATHER AND FOLLOWED HIS COMMANDS RATHER THAN THE PRACTICES OF ISRAEL. THE LORD ESTABLISHED THE KINGDOM UNDER HIS CONTROL; AND ALL JUDAH BROUGHT GIFTS TO JEHOSHAPHAT, SO THAT HE HAD GREAT WEALTH AND HONOR. HIS HEART WAS DEVOTED TO THE WAYS OF THE LORD; FURTHERMORE, HE REMOVED THE HIGH PLACES AND THE ASHERAH POLES FROM JUDAH.

Further into 2 Chronicles we discover large armies want to attack Jehoshaphat. The history here is that they hated David, and his descendants, so now they want to attack Jehoshaphat. **They want to show him right away what he's NOT—and to show him—and the people of Judah-they are more powerful. Many times... when you walk into something—the enemy will try and catch you off guard—just to try to point out that you're not good enough—your not strong enough—AND your not wise enough to do whatever it is that's been placed before you...to cause you paralyzing fear.**

Now these armies are coming after Jehoshaphat. They are intimidating armies- and could easily take Jehoshaphat and the people of Judah out. Eventually, they get word they're going to be attacked. Can you imagine how overwhelmed and trapped they felt? There was no way in the natural they could survive against such large armies. BUT GOD...

NOTES
_____
_____
_____

Praise is Our Best Weapon

Let's continue in Chronicles:

2 Chronicles 20:20-22 (NIV)

"EARLY IN THE MORNING THEY LEFT FOR THE DESERT OF TEKOA. AS THEY SET OUT, JEHOSHAPHAT STOOD AND SAID, 'LISTEN TO ME, JUDAH AND PEOPLE OF JERUSALEM! HAVE FAITH IN THE LORD YOUR GOD AND YOU WILL BE UPHELD; HAVE FAITH IN HIS PROPHETS AND YOU WILL BE SUCCESSFUL.' AFTER CONSULTING THE PEOPLE, JEHOSHAPHAT APPOINTED MEN TO SING TO THE LORD AND TO PRAISE HIM FOR THE SPLENDOR OF HIS HOLINESS AS THEY WENT OUT AT THE HEAD OF THE ARMY, SAYING: "'GIVE THANKS TO THE LORD, FOR HIS LOVE ENDURES FOREVER'

AS THEY BEGAN TO SING AND PRAISE, THE LORD SET AMBUSHES AGAINST THE MEN OF AMMON AND MOAB AND MOUNT SEIR WHO WERE INVADING JUDAH, AND THEY WERE DEFEATED.

They went to battle in worship and praise. Matter of fact, they thanked the Lord BEFORE the victory had even come. It's in the midst of our praise that our enemies will be defeated. Worship changes everything. Worship is our weapon, and in our darkest of times, worship is our lifeline. You may not immediately see the defeat of your enemy. However, if you succumb to this principal and praise and worship God through every battle, YOU *will be changed* and overcome with peace. Just as fear can be used as a weapon- *worship is the weapon God has given to you.* He has never left us unprepared to face hard times. He is with us and He will never leave us. That alone, is a reason to worship.

Just as fear can be used as a weapon- WORSHIP is the weapon God has given to you.

LET'S PAUSE

WHAT BATTLES ARE YOU CURRENTLY FACING?

_____
_____
_____
_____

HOW CAN YOU INCORPORATE REGULAR
WORSHIP TIME?

_____
_____
_____
_____

NAME A TIME WHEN YOU EXPERIENCED
GRATITUDE IN THE MIDST OF GREAT TRIAL.

_____
_____
_____
_____

In Closing

On this journey to *know God, and let go of fear*, we have been challenged through the life of Abram. Throughout this study, we were able to consider his life and his decisions and witness his humanity. In our time of reflection I hope this study has helped you to understand that even one of the great patriarchs experienced the same fears that many of us face today.

Genesis 12, was not the end of Abram's story. Eventually, he would become Abraham and would model great faith for future generations, consistently using his weapon of praise to combat doubt and fear. I encourage you after finishing up your study, to take some time to read the rest of Abraham's story in Genesis, where the promises God made were delivered.

Genesis 12:1 (NIV)

"I WILL MAKE YOU INTO A GREAT NATION, AND I WILL BLESS YOU; I WILL MAKE YOUR NAME GREAT AND YOU WILL BE A BLESSING."

Abraham became the father of the faith, with many descendants including the one that is our Messiah.

The Lord knows we are an imperfect people. He knows that many of us struggle with fear, anxiety, and so many other difficulties. However, God is a God of mercy. He has a great plan for each of us and my prayer for you is that this study has given you the tools to help fight the fears that plague you. Don't forget that the more time you spend with God, the more you will *know God*. The better you *know* Him, the more you will experience His peace.

Thank you for spending this time with me. I hope it has been helpful! If you are looking for other resources you can always find additional teachings at christywimber.com.

Christy

KNOW GOD
NO FEAR

You can follow Christy on Facebook, Instagram, Twitter, and Youtube.
christywimber.com

Made in the USA
Las Vegas, NV
28 November 2023

81709861R00031